thoughts of compassion .
with mett
07

MEMORIES of NATHANIE

- Peanut chili — YUM.
- Leather boots & miniskirts!

The Moon Appears
When the Water Is Still

- Stickies taped
all over Giannini
345, in prep. for
an all-nighter term
paper.

Reflections of the Dhamma

- Walks up to the botanical gardens...

Ian McCrorie

PARIYATTI PRESS, SEATTLE

Pariyatti© Press
P.O. Box 15926
Seattle WA 98115, USA

———————————————— Ω ————————————————

© 2003 Ian McCrorie

First Edition, 2003

All Rights reserved. No part of this book may be used or repro-
duced in any manner whatsoever without prior written permission
of Pariyatti Press, except in the case of brief quotations embodied
in critical articles and reviews.

ISBN 1-928706-17-7

Library of Congress Control
Number: 2002117330

Black & white photos by Andre Martel. © 2003 Andre Martel

The publishers gratefully acknowledge permission from Dover Pub-
lications, New York for use of the Japanese family crests that begin
each *Reflection*. They are from *Japanese Design Motifs: 4,260 Illustra-
tions of Heraldic Crests*, which is part of the Dover Pictorial Archive
Series.

Printed in Canada

Preface

During more than twenty years of intensive meditation in monasteries, ashrams and retreat centers in India, Southeast Asia, Japan and North America I have sat at the feet of numerous wise and charismatic elders and gurus. I have been inspired, set straight and at times admonished by their Dhamma talks. But it was not the long erudite lectures that cut through my mass of confusion. With my teacher, S.N. Goenka, a master of few words but many anecdotes, the light would go on when he related the right story at the right time. Often times it was but a sentence; a few times not much more than a word.

When he later appointed me to assist him by conducting meditation courses, I found myself resorting to these same allegories and metaphors, cutting to the chase so to speak, to make a pertinent point of the teaching clear to a student. Often, in answer to a student's question, I would say "It is as if…" not quite knowing with what metaphor, with what allegory or aphorism I would complete the sentence but trusting in the Dhamma to help. And sometimes I would hear later that whatever I had said had indeed dissolved the thick morass of confusion, just as similar allegories had done for me in years past.

So this little book is an offering of those stories, anecdotes and aphorisms that were an inspiration to me and to others. May they be so to you as well. Whatever truths are contained herein are of help when read or recalled at the time when they are most needed. I make no claim to originality; they are, after all, reflections. If you are thinking of starting a spiritual journey these reflections may inspire

you to take that first most important step. If you are a sea-
soned practitioner they may see you through those times
when the mind seems to get mired in the mud of doubts
and confusion. And I make no claim that these reflections
are factual; only that they mirror the teachings of the Buddha. A wise man once said that a story doesn't have to be
factual to be true.

Another equally wise man warned us not to mistake
the finger for the moon. We need the finger to point the
direction and we may be forever grateful for its clear guidance, but, after all it is only a finger; it is not the moon.
These reflections point to the Dhamma, they allude to the
truth, but the truth itself cannot be captured in words. It
can only be experienced. The words are mere Reflections
of the Dhamma.

The Moon Appears
When the Water Is Still

Reflections of the Dhamma

For my wife, Hyesun

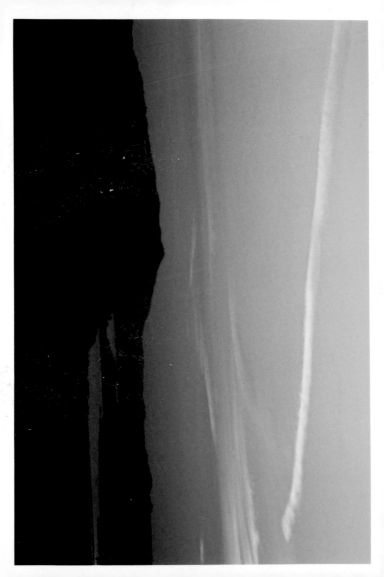

SF Bay from Berkeley

Sitting does not create truth,
meditation does not produce insight,
just as smelling a flower
does not make it fragrant.

The perfume of the rose is there.
We slow down to attend the unfolding
and flowering of its nature.
Slowing down and attending
to just this breath allows
the reality of Now to reveal its nature.

Sitting still gives us the opportunity
to witness the revealing of the truth.

The moon appears only when the water is still.

We sit through the storms
of pain and anguish.
We push on into the gale force winds
of our own resistance.
We strive to untangle the Gordian knots
of our karmic inheritance
until we faint from exhaustion
and finally give up.

It is only then,
when we see we can't do it,
that some insight
and some peace arises.
For the more we try,
the stronger become our enemies.
The more we sweat and strive
the deeper we sink
into the quicksand of our own craving.

We must make an effortless effort.
We have all the time in the world
but there is not a minute to lose.
To reach the final goal we must run fast
but never be in a hurry.

We can't do it but it can be done.

I am the cause of my own suffering.

Now 'tis true that the death of a loved one,
poverty, unrequited love, hunger
cause pain.
Pain is woven into the very fabric
of the human condition.
Even the Buddha could not escape pain.

I dislike this pain, I want it to cease,
I feel it is so unfair.
I forever dwell one-problem-removed
from divine bliss!

But still 'tis I and I alone who causes my suffering
for 'tis I and I alone who reacts to the inevitable
pain and malaise and discontent
of human life.

Pain visits all
but suffering comes not
to those who welcome its arrival.

We need not fear the arising of thoughts
only fear being too slow to notice them.
Once we take notice of any thought
the mind is then flooded with awareness
which swallows the thought. It can now be seen
for what it was before we reacted to it:
a harmless, simple verbal synapse.

Our job is not to eradicate thoughts
but to desist from reacting to them.
If the non-arising of thoughts is our goal
then rocks are enlightened.

Follow the leader who seeks not followers.
Heed the advice of one who offers none.
Obey strictly the teachings of he
who speaks highly of other paths.

Respect the guru whose self portrait
is absent from the walls.
Make offerings to one who charges not for any teaching.
Bow to one who asks you to refrain from such displays.

Surrender to the teacher who asks that you question
everything he says and does.
And love the teacher who seeks only
that you show your devotion by walking the path.

"My hut is leaking," said the novice,
"And my stairs are rickety."

"Wonderful!" replied the abbot.
"There is no need to thank me."

"We get the same food every day,
and not enough of it!"

"Excellent! Again no need to thank me"

"My hut is too close to the village
and I can hear their festivals."

"Perfect. No thanks necessary."

"I keep telling you how terrible everything is
and you keep saying it is wonderful."

"And it is wonderful.
The world just as it is
is all we need to achieve liberation.
Misery is the compost for the flowering of Dhamma.
Without imperfection, growth in Dhamma
would not be possible.
In a perfect world we can attain only complacency.
In an imperfect world we can attain enlightenment."

Before the rain ends,
a bird is heard.
Before the snow clears,
crocuses appear.
Before the storm ceases,
a rainbow is seen.
And before enlightenment,
there is sitting still.

There is no end to our meditation,
and no beginning to liberation.

We sit for what else is there to do?
Actions that stem from a clouded, confused mind
can never bring forth good.

Watering the apple tree with coal oil
produces only soot.

On a rainy evening a young monk came
seeking shelter.
"You are welcome to stay," replied the woman,
"But the barn is old and leaky.
Stay here in the house with me."

"I cannot do so for that would break my vow
of chastity."

"Then go next door and tell my neighbor
that my family has arrived
and ask if could I have his chicken
to make them a fine meal."

"I cannot do that for that would break my vow
of truth."

"Then go next door and kill the chicken
and I will cook it for us."

"I cannot do that for that would break my vow
to do no harm"

"Then go next door and bring the chicken to me
and I will kill it and cook it."

"I cannot do that for that would break my vow
to not steal."

"Then have a glass of wine with me
before you take rest."

"I cannot do that for that would break my vow
to avoid all intoxicants."

"But what harm can a small drink do?"
the woman asked.

The monk agreed.
And before the night was over all the vows
had been broken.

To think that you are mad
is sanity itself.
And to believe you are sane
is sheer madness.
Our habitual craziness is greatly enhanced
by the fear of madness.
Fear of the approaching storm
creates more sound and fury
than thunder and lightning ever could.

We remain quite normal
despite the inner turmoil.
Only the very sane can face this madness
with detachment and a smile
of resigned surrender.

The monk came home from the forest one day.
He met his friends, older now, and heard of their lives.
He met his family and shared in their joy and love.
He saw how the village had changed.

And then he met her.

He felt a stirring in his heart he had never known.
His bones and muscles turned to butter when she was near.
His tongue was of lead when he tried to speak to her.

And so he returned to the forest and to his master.
"I am a follower of the Dhamma, the law of nature.
I seek only the truth.
I want only peace.
How can I get involved in the mundane world
of a wife and a job and children?"

And his master said, "You can still follow the Dhamma,
the law of nature.
It is natural to love and to learn to do so without attachment.
You seek the truth.
And what is more honest than a life-long commitment
to another.
You want only peace.
And you can seek peace through this commitment
by developing equanimity."

And the monk returned home from the forest
for the last time.

The crazed one entered the town shouting,
"I have lost my head!
I can't find my head!"

The townsfolk caught hold of the man
and brought him to the elder.
The elder held up a mirror to the man.
"I've found it!" he shouted.

The townsfolk all laughed
as the crazed man
left their village
happy with his mirror.

"Why do you laugh?" the elder asked.
"You too are crazed.
You too look outside yourself
for what you already have!
All you need lies within you.
You search for happiness; it is in your heart.
You search for truth; it is in your mind.
You search for gold; it is in your smile.
You search for beauty; it is in your eyes.
You search for another to fulfill you,
when it is yourself you should seek!"

We think we need to get somewhere,
to reach that place of truth.
We see ourselves as devoid of purity,
and lacking in this or that virtue.
Yet this truth, purity and virtue are within us
momentarily obscured by our greed and hatred.
The sun remains the sun
obscured though it be by dark clouds.

Don't seek,
for there is no thing to grasp.
Don't try to get anywhere
for there is no where to get.
Where we need to be is here.
There is no there, there.
What we must do is find
what we must not look for.
What we seek we have already.

When we sit truly still
we have everything
because we are nowhere to be found.

In seeing the sunrise
just see it.
Do not be busy looking for the dawn.

"The war lord is coming!
Run for your lives!"
To a man the monks fled the monastery.
Only the aged abbott remained.

The war lord entered
the vacated monastery,
pleased that his reputation alone
could induce such fear.

He came upon the abbott
seated still in the meditation sanctuary.
"Do you know I could run this sword through you
without so much as batting an eye?"

"And do you know," replied the abbott
"That you could run that sword through me
and I wouldn't so much as bat an eye?"

The war lord sheathed his sword
and prostrated himself before the abbott.

Buddha and Māra
were out walking one day.
They passed a magnificent forest
wild, free and teeming with life.

"What is that?" asked Māra.

"Why, that's Truth," answered Buddha.

"Give it to me," replied Māra
"And I'll map it, organize it, catalogue it,
publish a book, open a web site,
and teach it at the university!"

No one liked the new chief monk.
He had a grating way about him
that tried everyone's patience.
He seemed argumentative and petty.

When questioned about his choice
The abbot smiled and said,
"Every meditation hall
needs a fly!"

The young man was a spiritual seeker
of serious intensity.
Nothing would stand in his way to enlightenment.

Through jungle, mountain and river
he traveled to obscure retreats, monasteries and hermitages
seeking out renowned masters and sages of high repute.
He sought to know what the truth was.

Many he questioned gave complex, learned answers.
A few remained in stony silence.
Only one, a kindly monk, deflected the question.
"I know nothing," the monk said.
"But in the village next is a simple cobbler.
Go to him. Stay with him. Watch him.
But don't ask him anything spiritual.
He will reveal to you great truths."

And so the young man apprenticed with the cobbler.
He never asked him anything spiritual.
And of such matters the cobbler never spoke.
Shoes came in and shoes went out.
All day they worked.
In the evening they sat outside
and watched the stars.

After many years the cobbler died.
From far and wide mourners came
for all knew him as a truly wise man.
The monk came to pay his respects.

Later he spoke to the seeker,
No longer a young man.
"I know you have found what you were seeking.
You are now the village cobbler.
Shoes come in and shoes go out.
I may send a young man to you one day.
He will be looking for the truth.
Let him work with you.
Do not tell him anything spiritual."

When one drop of rain
into the ocean falls
does it cease to be a drop?
Or is it now a part of a greater scheme?
Since its nature did not change
was it ever not a part of the ocean?

We are part of a greater whole,
linked by our humane-ness,
joined by our compassion,
entwined by our frailty.

When I scrape away the dust of delusion
and escape the individual illusion of I
the pain of the Somali child's hunger
brings an ache to my belly,
the frustration of the Afghani woman
causes a seething anger in me
and the smile of the Thai forest monk
melts my heart.

The problem of our human condition
is like that of a man with a broken finger
who experiences pain everywhere he touches.

Everywhere we touch we feel the pain
of sickness, of sorrow, of old age and death;
the pain of separation from loved ones;
the pain of unrequited expectations.
From these we cannot escape.
From these we need not escape.
We need only to fix the broken finger.

So place it in a splint of Dhamma,
soothe it with the balm of concentration
and wrap it with the bandage of kindness.

"Go find the Dhamma!"
the abbot demanded
of his three senior monks.

The first set off for the city
and returned the next day
with a gold-inlaid set of the Tipiṭaka,
the entire teachings of the Buddha.

"This is not the Dhamma," declared the abbot.

The second went deep into the forest.
There he found an old log
which he whittled into an exact replica
of the famous Kamakura Buddha.

"This is not the Dhamma," declared the abbot.

The third sat in his hut
unable to decide whether the Dhamma
was to be found in the forest or the city.
After ten days he gave up.

On his way to tell the abbot of his failure
he picked a lovely lotus flower.

"I confess I could not find the Dhamma," he said.
"I picked this beautiful flower to offer as a compensation,
but once out of the water it began to wither
and now it is dead!"

"In seeing this," declared the abbot
"you have found the Dhamma."

I approached her as much to enliven her day
as to make a purchase.
Though she spoke no English
she kindly presented to me her wares.
Carefully, unhurriedly, completely.
I bought a stack of postcards.
She smiled not, unimpressed I guessed
at my Western largesse.

Every day I went by her stall.
Every day I purchased more cards.
Every day I was met by the same placid demeanor.

She appeared neither happy when I engaged her
nor saddened when I left.
I craved a reaction from her
whether it be joy that I interject some life into her boredom
or anger at my persistent presence.

In time I came to understand
it was not indifference she displayed
but a deep peace
and a subdued joyous balance.
Selling or not selling was beyond her.
Her role was to be present to life itself
as it unfolded.
And to be aware of now, this moment,
without wishing or dreading it to be otherwise.

The monks entered the meditation hall
eyes downcast and in silence.
When the abbot entered they bowed as usual.
To their surprise the golden Buddha
that usually resided behind the abbott was missing.

"Find the Buddha!" roared the abbott.

The monks scattered;
all but Sumangala the novice
who worked in the kitchen.
He continued to sit in silence.

To a one, the monks returned
and admitted their failure.
"Do not fret," said the abbot,
smiling at Sumangala
"We have found our Buddha."

"Meditation," said the master,
"Is to quiet the mind.
Return to your hut
and sit until you are no longer
thinking of the white elephant."

The novice did so
sure of the simplicity of the task before him
for up to this point in his life
he had never thought of a white elephant.

For one hour he tried
to get rid of the thought
of the white elephant
but it persisted.
All day, all week, all month he tried
but the image of the white elephant
persisted in an increasing myriad
of confusing and unwanted images.

He returned to the master
and admitted his failure.
"To quiet the mind," the master said,
"Is not to quiet the activities on the mind.
It is to quiet our frustration with those activities.
The harder we try to stop the chatter,
the stronger it becomes.
Trying to stop the activities on the mind
is like putting out a fire
with gasoline."

Only with love can one know silence.
This quiet mind, the lotus flower heart,
at peace with all and sundry,
arises naturally from the pond of loving-kindness.

Let no meal go unshared
nor any gift unthanked.
Cast no one from your heart
for hatred can cease only with love.
My enemy's shadow is dark only because
the light deep inside is so bright.

My intellect deduces that I am nothing
but my loving heart tells me I am everything
and everyone.

We take inspiration from the Buddha
who sat always with a half smile,
bemused perhaps at how we complicate
something as simple as the truth.

Much like a man without hands
trying to make a fist;
don't push, don't strain,
don't even try to sit.
Just sit.

Enlightenment isn't something terribly holy,
just lots of space.

The master was very ill,
some said he was on the way out.
Too aged and fragile to move,
the doctors all said he must eat
to regain some strength
so he could be taken to the nearby hospital.

All manner of food was brought to him
exotic fruits from the islands,
rare rice from the hills,
special cheeses, silver-encrusted eggs,
all prepared by the finest cooks
and brought to him on golden trays
by his numerous and wealthy devotees.

But still he would not eat.
He slipped closer and closer to death.

A young boy from a poor family
came to hear of the plight of the master.
He walked all day to pay his respects.
He arrived and stood in a long queue of devotees
each bearing a special dish to revive the master.

As the poor boy got closer to the head of the line,
he grew ashamed for with him he had
but an old, shriveled apple
that he was saving for the journey home.
The boy had not eaten all day.

Finally he stood before the master.
He paid his respects
and placed the apple on the food altar.
The master's eyes opened just at that moment.
And he reached out his hand.

As his devotees stood in amazed silence,
he took the shriveled apple
and ate.
As he did so, his strength started to return,
enough to whisper these few words:

"A gift to be a true *dāna* must be
freely given without concern for merit.
Only one among you gave all he had.
Only this unconditional love
could convince me
to stay in this world a while longer."

In the jungle hunters place
a banana in a bamboo cage.
There is a hole just large enough
for a monkey's hand.
The monkey reaches in and grabs the banana.
Now he can't extract his hand.
He has trapped himself.
To go free he must simply let go of the banana.
But out of greed and ignorance, he holds tightly to
the very cause of his imprisonment.

Let go, let go, let go.

Meditation is a constant letting go.
Fears of pain, sickness and death,
let them go.
Thoughts of harm, rebuke and guilt,
let them go.
Images of Christ, the Buddha and my Teacher,
let them go.

But we cling.
We hold on to our unhappiness
like an abused puppy
who knows only one master.
The compass points to the true North
but with it we carry the two magnets
of greed and hatred
which skew the arrow.
Misery is our only friend
but we fear loneliness
more than we want peace.

We so want to be free
of our defilements and impurities
without understanding that we are addicted
to the excitement of these miseries.
We are like children who wish to be warm and cozy
but won't stop playing in the rain.

The Buddha has not gone anywhere.
You will see him every day,
in every gift you give,
in every lonely person you befriend,
in every homeless person you shelter,
in every naked child you clothe.
He is there
whenever you experience *Anattā*.

You will see him every day
in the tears of a child parting from his mother,
in the swollen belly of the refugee,
in the anguish of those trapped in prison,
in the death of a loved one.
He is there
whenever you experience *Dukkha*.

You will see him every day
in the budding of a tree,
in the return of the water fowl,
in the icing of the pond,
in the melting of the snow.
He is there
whenever you see *Anicca*.

Upon his release from prison
he made his way to his master.

"Did they starve you?" asked the master.
"Yes, they did," he replied.

"Did they isolate you?" asked the master.
"Yes they did," he replied.

"Did they make you renounce the Buddha?"
asked the master.
"Yes, they did," he replied.

"Did they torture you?" asked the master.
"Yes, they did," he replied.

"Were you afraid?" asked the master.
"Not of starvation, not of the isolation,
not of the mental reconditioning ,
nor of the physical pain they caused me," he replied.
"I was most afraid that I would lose
love and compassion for my imprisoners."

See the mountain as a river would;
hear the stream as a fish does
smell the smoke of a fire as the trees must
and touch the snow as only the wind can.

Beyond the ego of my "I"s
is the direct experience of this world
free of explanation, devoid of interpretation
and above any teaching.

I am the guide and the guided.
I am the walk and the walker.
I am the seer and the seen.

I am Buddha.

Perhaps it is time to sit less...
and meditate more.
Mindfulness is easy on the cushion,
difficult on the street.

But it is here, in the life,
in the body, in the to and fro
that we more clearly see our impurity
our delusion, our greed, and our hatred
and it is here we most need
to watch, to see, to be aware
to sit with it all,
to be with it,
to be.
We need to sit when we move.

Meditation is not an escape.
It is but the silent observation of reality.
And this can be done,
must be done
with every breath we make,
with every step we take.

At sunset the monk went to the jungle.
There he sat under a large tree,
closed his eyes and meditated.

From his stillness emanated feelings
of love, compassion and good will.
Late into the night a stray kitten
seeking some warmth and comfort
curled up in his lap and slept.

At daybreak when the monk roused himself
he was aware of some villagers approaching.
They paid their respects to the monk
and spoke thusly: "Venerable Sir,
a man-eating tiger attacked our village last night.
And we have followed his tracks to this spot.
There they end. Have you seen this tiger?"

"If you mean to kill this tiger,
then no I have not seen your man-eater.
If you mean to chase this tiger away,
then yes I have seen him.
He is behind you as we speak."

Upon hearing his roar
the villagers scattered in all the four directions.
Behind them stood the kitten.
"My honorable companion of the night
may you find sufficient food in this jungle
that you need not seek it in the village."

The tiger bowed and continued on his way.

Alone in the desert and
after weeks of meditation, prayer and fasting,
the carpenter from Nazareth
was visited by the Buddha.

"I am the Son of God," said Jesus.

"And so you are," replied the Buddha.
"For God is truth, kindness and wisdom
and you are the embodiment
of truth, kindness and wisdom."

"I am the Way," said Jesus.

"And so you are," replied the Buddha.
"For you have shown
by your word and your deed
the path to liberation from suffering."

"Whoever believeth in me
shall have everlasting life," said Jesus.

"And so it is," replied the Buddha.
"For whosoever follows the path
shall obtain *Nibbāna*."

"And who are you?" asked Jesus.

"I am your brother," replied the Buddha.
"We are born of the same mother, contemplation,

and our father was inspiration.
We were both born in the land of misery,
inspired by the seekers of truth who came before.
We both turned from our profession
to seek the answer to those most fundamental of questions.
And we leave our teaching
for those who will come after.

In time, some will come
who will say you and I are two.
For aeons these blind men will
lead many astray.
But a time shall come
when Truth will rule
and you and I again

They argued long into the night.
Which path was true?
Which texts were authentic?
Which school taught the pure Dhamma?

Late into the evening a servant boy
came bearing tea.
The load was heavy so
each step was carefully measured
and calmly taken.

"And what do you do here?" asked
one of the learned monks.
"I serve tea," answered the boy.

"Where are you from?"
"Here."

"When did you start work?"
"Now."

The servant boy smiled,
bowed and left.

"Perhaps," said the monk
"It is we guides who need
to observe one such as this
whom we hope to guide
for he understands more clearly than us
that the truth is
not seeking more answers
but asking fewer questions."

The master advised a raft to get to the other shore
where awaited a life of peace and clarity.
So the student researched the most buoyant logs.
He studied currents and tides.
He attended the preeminent building class.
and he perfected his stroke to take him
effortlessly across the watery expanse.

For ten, twenty and sometime thirty days
and for hours at a stretch he trained
up and down the river.
He grew into an excellent raftsman.
The idea of the perfect raft obsessed him;
the one and only vehicle
to cleanly navigate the treacherous waters.

His objective to reach the distant shore
was held in abeyance as he completed his book on rafts.
He freely gave of his time to attend learned conferences.
He was invited to lecture at prestigious institutions.
His many students took up the bulk of his time.

His master sat awaiting his arrival
but the distant shore remained unattained.

The essence of the Dhamma is meditation.
It leads us to the direct experience of the teachings.
It is the *sine que non* without which
the Dhamma is not much more than verbalization,
empty postulations and prostrations,
mere aspirations to noble ideals.

To remove meditation from the Dhamma,
and sit free of the teachings
is to abort the fetus of insight
before the birth of liberation.
Like removing gasoline from the automobile
and hoping the fuel source alone
is all we need to take us home!

Meditation is the mountain spring
that gives birth to the Ganges of Dhamma.
To capture and bottle this well-spring of the teachings
prevents the Dhamma
from ever gaining its full potential
to irrigate the deserts of suffering.

Friendship is not friendship
which dissolves when we are harmed
or slighted by those whom we hold most dear.

Let me judge myself and others
on the nobility of our intention
and see a friend as true indeed
who ever errs and lets me down
but whose heart is free of malevolence.
and whose mind knows not vindictiveness.

It is not the results or consequences
of our actions that require introspection
but our intentions.
I have little sway over the events
on the billiard table of life
but I can insure that my cue stroke
is honest and true.

Kindness is both the means to liberation
and the end.
It is a pre-condition and a result,
both path and fruition,
Alpha and Omega.

Before any real insight can be attained,
before even the first step can be taken
there must be kindness.
And when all the work is done
and all the impurities have been abandoned
all that is left is kindness.

Two monks came to a mountain stream.
There stood a beautiful young woman
too fearful to cross.
The elder monk picked her up
and transported her across the stream.

The monks continued on their journey,
the older monk serene, happy and content,
the younger monk perplexed and agitated.
Finally, he could contain himself no longer.

"How could you carry that woman across the stream?
We have taken a vow not to touch a woman.
How could you hold that woman in your arms?"

"Oh that woman?" the old monk said.
"I put her down after crossing the stream.
Why are you still carrying her?"

Silence is not quiet.
Quiet is the opposite of noise.
If you want quiet
go to a park.

Silence is the still mind
behind the quiet and the noise.
If you want to attain silence
sit.

If you seek quiet
from beginning to end,
then you are confused.
Nurture the still mind behind the noise
and then when quiet does come
it will be of little import.

Searching for quiet is like
scratching your foot
with your boot on.

In India I came upon a beggar woman
covered in dust and grime
seated at the side of the road.
Someone had given her a plate of food
which had attracted a mangy and growling mad dog.
He too was hungry
and without hesitation she shared
her only food with him.
He ate and then lay down at her feet.

Locked in their respective *kammas*
there was still room for kindness.
And if I could but speak her language
(I spoke unilingual affluence
and she all the dialects of abject poverty)
I would beg her to tell me
how her heart can shine so brightly
beneath the dust of her life.

The young novice returned
to his master after a year
in the forest alone.

"I am still lost in thoughts,
I miss my family and friends
and I can't quiet my mind.
I am miserable!"

"Good!" replied the master.

"How can that be good?"

"The first step to liberation is to experience
that suffering is inherent in being born."

"And the next step?"

"Is to realize that this suffering…"

"…is good?"

"No. Suffering is not good."

"What is good then?"

"The ability to observe the suffering is good."

"Good."

Our biggest problem
is trying to solve our problems.
Dhamma is not a way out of our problems
it is a way into them...and through them.
Meditation is a noun not a verb and often
the most important act is not acting.

This very same thinking process
that got us into this mess in the first place
cannot now extricate us from our predicament.
It is like trying to heal my burned hand
by pouring scalding water on it.

Our goal is not answers
but fewer questions.
Be attentive. Be present.
Hear the now.

The Dhamma is not a religion
　　　　though it is spiritual.
It is not a relaxation technique
　　　　though it is calming.
It is not a philosophy
　　　　though it is logical.
It is not passive
　　　　though it is equanimous.
It is not active
　　　　though it is energizing.
It does not strive
　　　　though it has a goal.
It does not profess a heaven
　　　　though there is salvation.
It speaks not of sin
　　　　though it has a moral code.
It admonishes grasping
　　　　though it is aspiring.

You need to abandon all hope
though you must have complete faith.

The mind is like an ice pond.
Though in essence it is all water
it needs the energy of the rays of Dhamma
to melt.

When ice melts, then water flows and moistens;
only then can it irrigate the fields of dried earth.

When the mind purifies, then thoughts are open and clear;
only then can it function with kindness and wisdom.

The Dhamma teaches us to be unattached.

If we sit twenty hours a day
in an isolated cave
at the top of the mountain
eating only fruits and berries
that have fallen from trees
and wearing only rags gathered
from waste sites,

yet,
we are full of pride to be living such a holy life,
then we have attached to our detachment.

We are wasting our time.

To abandon the mundane life
and attach to the holy life
is like jumping into fire
to avoid drowning.

Better it is to be aware that I am attached
Than unaware that I am unattached.
Worse still is to be attached to my awareness.

Craving is at the root of my problems.
Life is problematic only when
I crave it to be otherwise.

My separation from you is painful
to the degree that I crave to be with you.

My illness is suffering
to the degree that I crave to be healthy.

My old age is a misery
to the degree that I crave for my youth.

My death is feared
to the degree that I crave to live long.

Life is a great problem
when I try to sidestep it.

Only we humans want cows to fly;
The cows are content to graze.

Life is like bailing a boat with a hole in it.
No matter how fast we work,
no matter how large our pail,
no matter how many friends help us,
water continues to pour in.

But what if we accept the fact
that our boat has a hole in it
and sooner or later it will sink?

We continue to bail
without the hope of stemming the water
but because bailing is the stuff of life.
Now freed of the craving to solve
the tragedy of our existence
we can turn our eyes to the heavens above
and bask in the wonder and joy
of the futility of it all.

Don't worry—
things will get worse.

A few monks were leading a meditation session
on the eighteenth floor of a Tokyo office tower.
An earth tremor hit the building.
Glass broke. Alarms sounded.

To a one the students
sitting so composed a moment ago
fled the hall and rushed outside.

The monks bowed to the Buddha image,
stood and mindfully walked to the exit.
An earthquake was no excuse
to lose one's composure.

May I not practice what my teacher has learned
but learn what my teacher practices.

Enlightenment is naught else but
being awake.
I strive to be fully aware of each passing moment
and completely awake to every flutter
in the breeze of life.

And it surely is a breeze
For when the winds of craving have been abated,
the ego storms not,
nor the anger rage.

Awake. Aware.
Sitting still even as I move about.

You are a Christian.
For unexplainable reasons
the Christ speaks to you.
I don't understand it.
God chose a middle-aged carpenter
to be tortured on the cross
to save us from our sins.

I am a Buddhist.
For unexplainable reasons
the Buddha resonates with me.
I don't understand this either.
A Prince forsakes his duties and his family
to live the life of a beggar
to find the cause of suffering.

These are our chosen boats to cross
the river of human misery.
But to expect the Buddha or the Christ
to row our boats for us is folly.
We must do that ourselves and for that
we need the oars of Dhamma.
Understanding the universal law
of cause and effect
calms the forces of night
and permits love and kindness
to light our lives.

By meditating
we are like the candle
which says to the darkness
"I beg to differ."

Our quiet equanimity
says to the overly zealous
pontificators of opinions and views
"I beg to differ."

Our solitary renunciation
says to the perverted
promoters of sensual entertainment
"I beg to differ."

Our stellar resolve
says to the salacious
purveyors of instant gratification
"I beg to differ."

My meditation is a silent but powerful candle
saying to all the forces of darkness
"I beg to differ."

Happiness is what we seek,
but pleasure is where we look.

We are like the man who lost his keys
in the basement.
He looks for them upstairs
because there the light is better.
Those who search for happiness
only in the bright lights
are doomed to search in vain.

Like Nazruddin we keep eating chili peppers
waiting for a sweet one.

As a teacher of patience and tolerance
the Buddha was a failure.

He did not make problems for us.
He did not wish to harm us.
He did not bear us ill will.

It is our enemies,
of the internal and external kind,
who provide us with the opportunity
to grow in patience and tolerance.

Be thankful to those who hurt us
for they place the Dhamma before us.
We just need to open our eyes.

We are here to be a burden to one another.

We crave for peace of mind.
When unwanted thoughts impinge,
we crave to eradicate them.
The thoughts though are not the problem.
It is this craving to be at peace
which opens the door to agitation.

Difficult it is indeed to merely observe thoughts.
We get involved with seductive scenarios.
We run from terrifying replays.
We wish to end this addiction
of attraction and revulsion.
But it is this very wish
which further energizes the uninvited thoughts.

Wisdom springs forth not from thinking
but from clearly seeing
this craving we have
to be free of agitation.
The thinker is one person.
The one who watches is another.
Get to know him.

My hang dog expression
reflected the burden of family and future
I carried.

No friends had I
to help me over the hurdles.
No mentor had I
to ease my volatile mind.

Wrapped in the enigma of ego delusion
the great "I" rolled on in selfish scenarios.

One day I came upon a child
playing in the sun.
I smiled. He smiled.
My mind calmed for a moment.
Was it his smile or mine
which stilled the storm?
Whose smile made whom smile?

Regardless, I continued to smile
and the increasing joy I felt
was reflected back to me ten-fold.
I saw that my happiness is inexorably entwined
with your happiness.
Only by watering your joy
can mine blossom.

When I see to it that you are happy
my happiness is automatically enhanced.
As I wash my right hand
My left also gets cleaned.

The path begins with kindness.
The ten *paramīs* are
extensions of kindness.

We are kind to others when we keep our
MORALITY pure.

We show kindness when we develop our
WISDOM so that we can guide others.

We are kind when we grow in
RENUNCIATION so that we do not over-consume.

We exemplify kindness when we practice
EQUANIMITY so that we remain calm and balanced
under pressure.

We kindly encourage ourselves to be
GENEROUS to give to others what they need.

We display our kindness when we show
LOVE to all beings.

We are being kind when we make
EFFORT to constantly try to improve our behavior.

We are acting with kindness when we let the
TRUTH guide our words and deeds.

It is a kind act to be
TOLERANT of others and not to discriminate.

And finally we are being kind when we develop
STRONG DETERMINATION to not abandon
any of the other nine *paramīs*.

The student approached his master.
"I request most humbly to move
deeper into the forest.
I hear the noise of the nearby village
and the sound upsets me."

"'Tis you," replied the master,
"Who is upsetting the sound.
The sound is just a sound
free of any intention to harm or soothe.
Leave it alone. Stop bothering it.
Let the sound get back to sounding.
You get back to hearing.
Just hearing."

"I feel you have not given me enough guidance."

The teacher remained silent.

"You've left me totally on my own."

Still there was silence.

"I have had to do all the work myself."

Again silence.

"All you gave me was time to discover the truth for myself."

Still silence.

"But I guess in the long run this was the best way."

Silence.

"I am honored that you respected me enough
to let me discover the truth on my own."

The Dhamma is not a way out of our problems
but a way into them.

In our problems we realize the futility of thinking.
In our problems we experience
the pain of the human condition.
In our problems we see the cause of our misery.
And in our problems we see that we are that cause.

The Dhamma takes us into this morass
and through it.
The Dhamma is more bridge than detour!

A wise saint once said,
"As ye sow, so shall ye reap."

If we plant seeds of anger, jealousy, or hatred
we will harvest only weeds of sadness and misery.
Such is the universal law of nature.
Day follows night. Fathers beget sons.
The apple not only falls close to the tree
the apple is the tree.
Seeds of kindness watered with smiles
must produce flowers of happiness and joy.

The Dhamma teaches you to be selfish.
Think only of your own happiness
and strive ceaselessly to increase it.

But as you grow in wisdom it becomes clearer
and clearer
that your happiness is inexorably linked to others.
Your happiness cannot increase at the expense of others
nor can you remain unhappy
as those around you abound in joy.
Though you be naked, homeless and hungry
if the happiness of others is paramount
you will be clothed, sheltered and fed
with a joy beyond compare.

But without wisdom to guide you
though you attain everything in the world
your only true possession will be misery!

Be selfish.
Do all you can to increase
the happiness of others.

We must first realize
that life is quite unsatisfactory.
Unhappy events linger forever,
happy times vanish in the blink of an eye.

We must accept this condition.
Life begins with the pain of birth
and ends with the pain of death.
And between the alpha and omega
lives dis-ease.

Have faith that there is a way out
which is to understand that
the cause of this unsatisfactoriness is
craving.
We want the happy times to linger forever
and the unhappy events to vanish in the blink of an eye.

A life free of pain is not possible
but a life free of craving for it to be otherwise
is.
Once free of craving, though the pain remains,
the suffering ceases.

Long ago in a small clearing in a forest
lived a wealthy man.
A road frequented by robbers and smugglers
passed in front of his home.
Oft times they asked to stay the night.

Fearful of violent reprisals if he refused
he invited them to stay as long as they wished.
"My house is large with many rooms."
He ordered his servants to treat them well.
But at his table he placed but one chair
upon which he alone sat.

He smiled at his guests, wished them no ill will,
was gracious and generous
but ever watchful lest they rob or harm him.
He learned much of their sly and cunning ways.
He smiled at their unpleasant and worrisome overtures
and at their intriguing suggestions of easy wealth.
Never did he take his eyes off them.
Never was he swayed from his chair
and never did they join him at his table.

In time the brigands tired of staying there
for they realized they could not outwit the man
and they never returned.
But so trained to observe the guests in his house was he
that even when wealthy merchants asked to stay
he remained ever-watchful

lest they entice him into supporting their schemes.
And he continued to place but one chair at his table.

It was said that his home glowed
from all the gold which he had protected
from brigand and merchant alike.

No suffering is as unjust as my own.

I seek a reason for this unwanted, unreasonable state.
Who or what has caused my discomfort?
Perhaps parents, maybe enemies.
Then again perhaps my employer
or my genetic predisposition.
I must have been abused by someone
for surely I am entitled to eternal bliss.

Pointing my finger everywhere but inwards
I dwell forever in anger, frustration and resentment.
But liberation lies beyond recrimination.

I have been shot by a poisoned arrow.
What difference who shot it
or from where or with what bow.
Remove it.

Buddhaṃ saraṇam gacchāmi
We are sure that inevitably
we too will realize full liberation
as the Buddha, the fully enlightened one,
did so long ago.

Dhammaṃ saraṇam gacchāmi
We are sure that the guidance we receive
about the universal truths
is helpful and correct.

Saṅghaṃ saraṇam gacchāmi
We are sure that this is the right path
from the examples set by the community of elders
who have liberated themselves before us.

Buddha, Dhamma, Saṅgha

Like a once-drowning man
we have scrambled onto this raft of the *Saṅgha*
with a map given by the *Buddha*
and the strong wind of *Dhamma*
to take us safely to the far shore.

We need naught else to work out
our own salvation.

Be thankful for all transgressions
bestowed upon you by enemies or fate.
Return every abuse with a smile,
pay for each insult with a gift.

A wonderful opportunity to practice
forgiveness and understanding has been gifted.
Only the hurt can hurt; only the angry can anger.
Who but those previously abused, abuse?

It is not the grace of God that keeps me from going there;
I am already there, one with my transgressor,
enmeshed in human misery.
But with thanks I choose not revenge but tolerance.

When the heart opens there are no strangers.

When I am angry I go fishing to hook
he who has angered me.
But my anger has already caught me.
My agitated mind indicates
that I am truly the first victim of my anger.
When I feel a tug on my line
I think, "Now I've got him!"
But it's only me I have hooked.

Anger is like holding a two-edged sword
by the blade and lashing out with the handle.
I am the only one bleeding.

Do not seek a loving guide
until you see him in everyone.
And when you see him in everyone
what need is there for a guide?

When we are devoid of kindness
we cannot see it in others.
When we are lacking in love
we find only hatred and anger.

When a pickpocket sees the Buddha
he sees only pockets.

One monk said to his companion,
"It is so good to walk alone."
Replied his companion,
"Precisely. It is so good to be with you!"

This is Dhamma.
Total aloneness and total intimacy.
When I walk by myself
everyone is with me
And when everyone is walking with me
I am alone.

To make good things start
and bad things stop
the greatest aid is being still.

Stop trying to start the good
and start trying to not stop the bad.

No starting, no stopping,
only ever-progressing stillness.

The Dhamma is closest to those with broken hearts.
Only when your home has been burned to the ground
can you see the stars.
Do not throw away your suffering;
it is the fertile soil which grows the flowers of truth.

Embrace your pain
and share your pleasure.
Pain is the teaching,
release is the graduation.

The master came upon his student
circumambulating the pagoda and ringing a bell
upon each completion.
"What are you doing?" inquired the master.
"I am seeking full enlightenment" said the student.
"Better to practice pure Dhamma," replied the master.

Later, the master again encountered his student.
This time he was studying the scriptures.
"What are you doing?" asked the master.
"I am seeking full enlightenment," replied the student.
"Still it is better to practice pure Dhamma."

And a third time the master chanced upon his student
who this time was deep in meditation.
"Now what are you doing?" asked the master.
"I am seeking full enlightenment," replied the student.
"Much better to practice pure Dhamma," said the master.
"But what more can I do?" asked the student in desperation.

"Let go."

"My teacher is certainly enlightened.
He can sit on this side of the river
and write a note on the other side!"

"My teacher can perform an even greater miracle.
When he sits on this side of the river,
he is aware he is sitting on this side of the river.
And when he sits on the other side of the river,
he is aware he is sitting on the other side of the river."

After years of solitary meditation deep in the forest
the student returned to report on his progress
to his master.

"I have fasted, gone without sleep and
meditated long and hard," he reported,
"And now I can walk on water!"

"What a waste of time," replied the master,
"When there is a perfectly good boat nearby!"

The individual waves travel to their destination
and crash eventually upon the shore.
This is their destiny, but not their end
for they are pushed out again
to repeat the cycle.
They are not individual waves
as much as they are ocean.

If you can't do the right thing
or don't know what the right thing is,
simply do the next thing
with as much clarity, gentleness and kindness
as you can muster…
and then forgive yourself
when you are dead wrong!

To smell the Dhamma is to inhale a cloud.
To see the Dhamma is to glimpse night's shadow.
To hear the Dhamma is to listen to the mountain's song.
To touch the Dhamma is to feel the breath of summer rain.
To taste the Dhamma is to sip the dew from a lotus.

Difficult indeed is it to find the proper words
to capture the Dhamma.
It cannot be expressed but it can be experienced.

The Dhamma does not answer the big questions.
It removes them from the forefront of the mind
and allows the wisdom of letting go to ascend.
Then it's possible to know without answers
and to be wise but devoid of knowledge.
For knowledge, we acquire.
For wisdom, we let go.

The mountain stream knows but cannot answer.

Take all the sadness of your life
into your left hand
and all the joy
into your right.
It takes both these hands
to hold the truth.

Accepting only the good
and rejecting the bad
is like trying to breathe
taking only inbreaths.

I feel much better
now that I have given up hope.
I have accepted the fact
that I'm never going to get it all together.
I am content forever to be just
one need short of divine bliss.

I went for a walk
along an old trail
that wound around the mountain
behind a small Marāṭhī village.

As I crested a hill
I was stopped short
by an approaching herd of buffalo
returning from the high grasslands

No escape was possible.
At the sides of the trail
there lurked snakes.
To turn and run
might incur a stampede.
I stood still and closed my eyes
and was immediately engulfed
by the thundering herd.

However, I was not trampled nor impaled.
The beasts shifted their enormous carcasses
To avoid crushing me.
I was aware of the heat from their bodies
as they slowly swayed by me.
That they could easily trample me was evident.
That they had no need to was also clear.
I posed no threat to them.
And slowly I saw they posed no threat to me either.

They were just being buffaloes,
very stupid and somewhat awkward.
They were not aware of the strength they held
nor of the fear they could induce.

Later sitting still in my meditation cell
I faced the slings and arrows of my outrageous mind.
These intrusions too are not aware of their fearsomeness
nor how much I detest their incursion
into my peace and serenity.
They are just being impediments, stupid and awkward,
which stampede when we run from them
and are strengthened when we seek escape.
Face the buffalo.

I have travelled much, through desert and mountain
and have returned home to regale friends with stories
which increased in danger and daring with each telling.

But the best part of every trip
was to see friends and family again
with a renewed appreciation for the simple acts
of sharing a cup of tea with those you love.
The mundane life I fled so many years before
took on a soft, gentle hue
unbeknownst to me in times past.

And now I can safely say
that the greatest adventure
is not to explore new lands
but to explore the familiar landscape
with a new perspective.

During intensive meditation many mind states arise:
boredom, anger, jealousy,
fear, loathing, craving.
They all visit sooner or later.

But if one is patient,
if one allows them some space,
we notice that they will arise,
stay a while
and invariably pass on.

They are not so fearsome.
They are only as powerful
as we fear them to be.

By throwing sticks at barking dogs
we excite them more.
Smile, let them do what dogs do,
and their barking, let alone their bite,
ceases.

"I'm not yet ready to start meditating.
Too much have I on my mind.
I'm working through an issue with my wife
and I'm burning over something at work.
I need to wait until my mind settles down
until I have some peace."

My teacher smiled.
"In time these issues will settle down
but new ones will arise to replace them.
To wait for peace before one begins
the search for truth
is like waiting to graduate
before one learns to read.

We see our life through a glass, darkly.
It is not our life that need cleaning,
but the glass itself.
We can wait forever for the sun to cool;
better to wear a broad hat."

I prefer the word "sitting" to "meditating."
Meditating may be seen as another thing we do,
an activity, a practice, an engagement.
It might be a hobby or a game.
Sitting is non-active, it is a non-practice.
It is accepting, open, observant,
free from judgment.
It is an occasion to be mindful of the reality,
within and without us
and to be at peace with that reality.

It is the ultimate act of courage:
to not run away.
We do not seek escape.
We sit.

Wherever we are, it is elsewhere we long for.
Whomever we are with, it is others we long for.
Whatever we have, it is something else we long for.
It is hopeless.
This craving for other-than-it-is continues unabated.
But this is not mind, just a condition of mind.
Peace is stepping back from this perpetual penduluming
to see this craving for what it is:
insatiable discontentment.

Step back.
To see the beauty of the painting we must step back.

Oft times I would come to my teacher
With complaints about my pain.
"Don't fret," he would say "It may get worse!
And it may not go away."

Accepting that this pain
might be a permanent condition
was strangely comforting.
Free now of wanting to get rid of this attack on my peace
the pain would retreat.

Gruff and seldom smiling
my father did not suffer foolishness gladly.
He spoke little, laughed less,
focusing most of his affection on his automobile.

Late one after-party evening
I crashed this most proud possession.
I remained awake for what was left of the night
until I heard his slippers trundle to the kitchen.

He sat at the kitchen window
sipping his pre-beer coffee.
With trepidation I approached him,
my exhaustion playing up my fear
of his impending wrath.

I told him of the accident quickly.
I braced myself for the coming storm.
"Were you hurt?" was all he asked.

And it was then
for the first time
I met my father.
I wondered where he had been hiding
those past eighteen years.

But it was not he who was hiding but I.
I hid my love for him behind my anger
at his taciturn nature.

That morning so long ago
his simple question uncovered my love
and I saw that my father's love had always been there.
Those without love in their own hearts
are destined to search for love from others through eternity.

Look not at my actions, harmful though they were;
nor to my words which caused you great hurt.
Mulling these over in the mind rekindles your remorse.
See the intention behind these actions and words.
Therein lies the truth that must be judged
for only an intention to harm or hurt is wrong.

I do not seek your forgiveness,
but you do need to forgive.
I do not crave your love,
but you do need to love.
I do not want your compassion,
but you do need to be compassionate.

Without forgiveness, love and compassion
misery will follow you around
as surely as the cart follows the horse.

Anger is stimulated by events and people outside
but it resides deep within
and surges forth when our ego view is challenged.
Insults thrown our way, opinions thrust at us
are not the problem
as much as our reaction to those insults and opinions.

These attacks remain so much sound and fury
truly signifying nothing
when we maintain our balance.

Odd it is that while in a foreign country
words of abuse fall on deaf ears
and leave us unperturbed
despite the same intention to upset.
Abuse which goes unanswered remains
with the abuser.

Be deaf to the insults of others,
and blind to their actions.
Stay within.
Tune into the stockpile of reactive anger
residing there
and do nothing.

Where are these hell realms of which the Buddha spoke?
They exist in the fettered mind, the agitated mind,
the undisciplined mind that seeks pleasure
rather than happiness,
and finds fault with interrupted ecstasy.

The hell realms are found residing in the mind
that zaps from channel to channel seeking
to obliterate boredom.
They fester and multiply when virtual reality
replaces reality
and they arise when intoxicants are sought
to eradicate every discomfort.
The hell realms shout, "I want it to be otherwise!"

Hell realms are omnipresent when we crave for what we
don't have.

I had seen pictures of Dhammagiri,
a meditation center in India…
pristine, lush, tranquil and secluded.
When I arrived there to meditate
for a long period of time
its beauty more than surpassed the pictures I had seen.
Paradise.

I began to sit and soon the impurities of mind
were fighting for control.
I walked the paths of Dhammagiri with eyes down cast,
despondent and agitated,
my discomfort surpassed by anything I had imagined.
Hell.

What had changed Dhammagiri from paradise to hell?
None else but I was guilty.
I had created my own hell out of a paradise…
and I was determined to create my own paradise
out of this hell.

Mind matters most.

His life was an unparalleled success.
He worked long and hard but
no craving went unfulfilled.
He maintained a better car than all his friends;
a finer house, a more beautiful partner, more sumptuous food.

In time his acquisitive life paled
and he sought a simpler place
free from endless pursuits of the latest rage.
He sought escape from being number one.
He shaved his head and left for the monastery
deep in the woods.
He had nothing but discarded and torn robes to wear
and a rusty begging bowl to garner food.

On his first day as he stood in line
waiting for whatever foods the villagers
wished to place in his bowl,
he noticed the monk beside him
had a new, shiny stainless steel bowl.
His mind filled with jealousy and rage
and he plotted how he too could get such a bowl.

Craving is craving whether it is to rule the world
or to own a simple steel bowl.
Craving causes misery.
He who leads the holy life
is he who is free from craving
not he who has donned the robe
and dwells in secluded woods.

To free the mind we need not renounce
our jobs, our cars, our homes.
We need to renounce attachment.

When the darkness leaves, there is light.
When we relinquish the impurities,
and all that we cling to,
we are left with purity.
There is nothing to get, to acquire;
no state to which to attain.

We are not developing, as much as we are releasing.
We are not going anywhere, as much as we are leaving.
We are not acquiring, as much as we are letting go,
and we are not achieving, as much as we are
surrendering.

Our load of impurities is heavy.
We don't need to develop strong muscles to carry it.
We need simply to put it down.

The young goat herder
saw the Buddha sitting under a tree.
Enchanted by his serenity,
he approached the Buddha and asked,
"Are you a God?"

"No," replied the Buddha. "I am not a God."

"Are you then a man?" he asked.

"No," replied the Buddha. "I am not a man."

"Then what are you?" asked the boy.

"I am awake!" said the Buddha.

Deep in the forest in the heat of summer
we chose to meditate outside in the evening.
We were visible through the trees by our neighbour,
who was very opposed to our heathen ways.
To show her displeasure and convert us to her views,
she moved her drum set outside
and commenced practice as soon as we sat down.

As a novice I was resentful of this incursion
into my tranquillity.
I hated her for her hatred!
I noticed the other monks
didn't seem to be bothered by the tumult.
They talked of the *kyasaku*, a stick used in Zen practice,
to keep meditators awake and alert.
This then was to be our *kyasaku*
and we should develop great thanks for its help.
After each evening sitting we would privately
thank the neighbour for strengthening our practice.

I left the monastery soon after
but I have noticed that every meditation hall,
every temple, every retreat,
has an inadvertent drummer to keep us awake and alert.
Be thankful.

We were sitting in the meditation hall
all two hundred of us locked into our struggle
to maintain focus and balance
save for one very agitated man
who saw in our group effort
a conspiracy of control.

Swayed by his delusion
and spurred on by his rage,
he rushed at our teacher
shouting warnings and brandishing a large club.

Too late for any of us to protect him,
our teacher, seated quietly at the front,
opened his eyes and began quietly
to chant words of peace and love.

As the agitated man raised his club to strike
the vibrations of love and compassion
thrust him back from the dais
and he dropped his club.

How pretentious it was
to think we could protect our teacher
better than his loving kindness.
To be safe in this world
walk softly but carry a big heart!

We must start from where we are
not from where we want to be.
For where we want to be
is to be content with where we are.

We may be in hell
but if we are patient and
allow hell to just be hellish
then this balance of mind,
this quiet contentment
changes hell into heaven.

The one-sixteenth of an inch difference
'twixt heaven and hell
is equanimity.

List of first lines